# Florida's North Shore Diet

JAMES GREENE

AuthorHouse™
1663 Liberty Drive
Bloomington, IN 47403
www.authorhouse.com
Phone: 1-800-839-8640

Published by AuthorHouse 05/01/2014

ISBN: 978-1-4969-1076-9 (sc)
ISBN: 978-1-4969-1077-6 (e)

authorHOUSE®

*Dedicated to my lovely wife Jane*

# SILENT BUT DEADLY

We all know what this means and for those who don't, listen up.

During the time I was 9 or 10 years old, a group of us kids were outside playing and someone farted. It was one of those quiet ones that nobody heard and it smelled so bad it would take the paint off the wall. It was so bad no one claimed it. Everyone just took off running, hence "Silent But Deadly" or SBD. There are many things SBD could mean, but we used it for this.

This story started about 50 years ago when it was cool to smoke. Being the first in my neighborhood to steal a cigarette from an older family member, all of us who dared to had a puff. Mike and Fred did not. They did not feel it was right. If I had only known what I was doing, I would not have lit my first cigarette. A few weeks later I started to inhale. A slow but steady addiction had started. Before I even knew it, I was hooked. I had no clue what I was doing. I just wanted to be cool. Over the next 46 years I smoked every day. In no time I was up to one pack a day. In the Army I went up to 2 packs a day. It got so bad I could not hit my target unless I had a cigarette hanging from my mouth. Then, one day I was finished with the Army. Bored with life I hit 3 packs a day. I was addicted, I mean I was really, really hooked. Could not quit if my life depended on it, and it did; it really did!

I tried to quit several times, but at best it only lasted two days. Then I started to eat, figuring if I was eating I couldn't smoke. I started to gain weight. Now I was a fat smoker. This went on until I was 57.

One day I felt ill and the whole room started to spin slowly in full circles, just like in the movies. I had to lie down on the bed to keep from falling. The spinning stopped in about 4 or 5 minutes. Never been to a doctor's office since I had left the Army, except once when I had a sore throat. Not thinking that it was serious I put it aside. Then, it happened two more times, so I went to the doctor. He thought I might have something wrong with my brain and sent me to get a MRI. It came back as negative.

My doctor told me I had to, not should, but had to quit smoking and prescribed Chantex. He told me how to take it and what to look out for. You know the side effects. It was a miracle, to take a pill for one week and be able to quit smoking. One week went by, then another and another. This went on for 5 weeks. I did this against doctor's orders, you know, about taking

Chantex for one week then stop. I felt this is my only chance to quit. But you see, deep down inside of me I did not want to quit.

One day the cigarette tasted so bad and I had a chest pain. I put the cigarette out and will never lit one again. I had all the side effects, but didn't care because this was my last hope to quit smoking. I even kept a pack in my car just in case. I have been smoke-free for five years and just threw the pack away about two years ago.

This first doctor sent me to a second and he sent me to a third. Finally a cardiologist, yea, saved the day. This doctor literally saved my life. He found a 100% blocked artery, not just an artery. It was my carotid artery. Now my brain is being fed by one artery. The final closing of the artery caused the spinning and the visual things that started all of this. I get light headed a little but I am alive. The Silent But Deadly has now changed to Should Be Dead.

This doctor gave me a stress test, ultrasound and checked my blood for cholesterol levels which came back very high. The LDL was over 350. He told me I needed to lose some weight and get the LDL cholesterol down to 80 to 100 to be safe. He prescribed Crestor 10mg once a day. Three months went by and he checked again. The LDL was down to 224, still too high. He then put me on 20mg and in 6 months we checked it again. It's down to 160, close! But, this is still too high. One more time, I was up to 40mg once a day. Now were talking. The LDL finally went down to 70. I can live with that! I asked him why we did it that way. The doctor told me you should not start out at 40mg as it will mess your liver up. I am shooting for 50-60 but I do not know if it will go that low. My LDL cholesterol (lousy cholesterol) is finally under control. Thank you very much for giving me a second chance.

At first I thought all you had to do is take Crestor and it would do its job. How wrong I was! After that I changed my diet. All went well. It took a bit of time to get it right. I was in really bad shape, having smoked for 46 years. COPD a clogged carotid artery plus not eating the right foods with no exercise was the problem. Years of sitting in front of my computer surfing the internet and playing games compounded the problem. I got really good at saving the universe and protecting the earth, yea right. To sum it up this combined effort of life style put me in a really bad state of health.

Eating at fast food restaurants I hate to say, is definitely out. Almost everything on the menu has cholesterol, and lots of it. So what do you do? You keep track of the cholesterol value and how many servings it has in the package to start with. Let say the cholesterol value is 7% per serving, but, it has 2.5 servings. That means in the whole package it has 17.5% for a 2000 calories diet. It adds up fast. Sometimes math is necessary. What I do is choose 0% to 3% cholesterol. It is better math and it is better for you. Watch your cholesterol count!!

What I have done is come up with a list of foods and their cholesterol value. Spending many years trying different cholesterol free or low cholesterol foods, I have managed to make some meals for the day. This one is good if you do not have a weight problem. This diet can be all you can eat. It tastes really good and for me, that is important. We start this menu out with zero cholesterol days and work our way to days where some cholesterol is between 3% and 12% is allowed. Each day will have Breakfast, Lunch, Dinner and a Snack. You can skip lunch or the snack or eat smaller portions depending on your life style. You can substitute or trade anything you like as long as you watch the cholesterol levels. For the first week it would be zero. Fat percentages are listed if someone is watching their weight. All spices are on the table because they have 0% cholesterol and 0% fat. My pictures may not have added things like olives, parsley, cilantro, chives, lime and oranges that are not listed in the ingredients. Everything used is 0% cholesterol free for the first week. All sautéed foods are sautéed in Home Churned Buttery Spread. This is a butter substitute or margarine that has 0% cholesterol and 0% fat. Using other ingredients can be used as long as they all have 0% cholesterol for the first week, then the percentage value for that week. It will also change the calorie count, so keep this in mind when using substitutes.

Taking a multi-vitamin is recommended as not all vitamins and minerals are in these dishes. There dishes are designed to reduce your cholesterol only and do not have all the daily vitamins and minerals needed. It does not count salt, sugar or protein and it only counts cholesterol fat and calories.

In this diet we have started with cholesterol free meals for the first week. These are carefully made up breakfast, lunch, dinner and a snack. As you can see there is no meat or dairy products as they all have cholesterol. In the days to follow we added meat and dairy products in small portions but not to be more then the percentage for that period in one day. This diet starts the process of cleansing the body of cholesterol and will make you feel better about your health. All food percentages are before cooking. If you deep fry it will add to the percent of fat and calories.

# FOOD HIGH IN CHOLESTEROL

## YOU SHOULD DO NOT EAT ANY OF THESE TOP TEN

#1)  Egg
     One egg has approx. 71% DV

#2)  Caviar
     One tablespoon has 31% DV

#3)  Liver
     One tablespoon has 7% DV

#4)  Butter
     One tablespoon has 10% DV

#5)  Shrimp
     One oz has 18% DV

#6)  Fast Food Breakfast
     One An egg & sausage biscuit has 87% DV

#7)  Oil packed fish sardines
     has 44% per can 6% per sardine

#8)  Cheese
     One inch cube has 7% DV

#9)  Processed Meat
     has 21% DV per one link (approx)

#10) Shellfish
     has approx 10% DV

Most people eat 1 ½ servings, this chart is a small portion of the food, i.e.: cheese one inch cube. Not very many people will eat just one cube.

# FOOD THAT LOWER YOUR CHOLESTEROL
## YOU SHOULD EAT THESE TOP FIVE

#1)   Oatmeal, oat bran and high in fiber foods

#2)   Fish and omega-3 fatty acids; Salmon & Halibut

#3)   Almonds and walnuts

#4)   Olive oil

#5)   Fruit like Orange Juice and Yogurt

Next and last, before we get into the meals that you should be eating. This book is divided into 4 chapters. Each chapter has its limits in cholesterol intake. Here we look at fast carbs and slow carbs. Fast carbs make the blood sugar level spike and set your body into fast storage mode. Slow carbs do not set you body into this mode. When you eat more slow carbs then fast you lose weight and if you want to gain weight you eat more fast carbs then slow. It's that simple.

| FAST CARBS | SLOW CARBS |
| --- | --- |
| Bread | Beans |
| Pasta | Peas |
| Rice | Tomato |
| Corn | Onion |
| Potato | Bell Pepper |
| Milk | Broccoli |
| Cereal | Cooked Kale |

# CHAPTER ONE

## ZERO CHOLESTEROL WEEK

# BIG

## BREAKFAST

Coburn Farm Eggzactly as much as you want, this is egg white and flavoring. It tastes really close to the real deal. It makes for a great scramble egg dish.

You can add any vegetables you want. I like it with mushroom, onions, tomato, and garlic. Maybe a few black olives all chopped up and cooked it Home Churned Buttery Spread. Sautee the veggies in buttery spread in a separate pan.

Total about 100 calories per two eggs subs depending on how much butter spread and veggies you use.

Toast with Home Churned Buttery Spread & Smucker's Blueberry Preserves
All dressed up with a few fresh whole blueberries on top.
Total 130 calories per slice and 13% fat

Hash brown's cook in Home Churned Buttery Spread
Total 70 calories and 0% fat per patty

Florida's Natural Orange Juice as much as you want
Total 110 calories 0% fat per 8oz glass

## TOTAL CHOLESTEROL 0%, ZERO, ZIP, NADA & UNDER 500 CAL.

# BIG

## LUNCH

Corn or Flower Tortilla Refried Beans with Picante Sauce, Spanish rice and a Soda regular or diet

Flour Tortilla 8" 120 calories 4% fat Note; corn tortilla cooked in corn oil. Put in skillet turn over immediately and fold, turning the folded tortilla often.

Old El Paso Refried Beans 90 calories 12% fat per ½ cup

Pace Pecante Sauce 10 calories 0% fat per 2 Tablespoons

Lettuce, tomatoes, onions and taco sauce to taste

Zatarain's Spanish Rice 180 calories 0% fat per 1 cup

Hunt's Diced Tomatoes mixed with rice 35 calories 0% fat

Soda 140 calories

## TOTAL CHOLESTEROL 0%, ZERO, ZIP, NADA & UNDER 600 CAL.

# BIG

## DINNER

Spaghetti and Prego Paste Sauce, use Roasted Garlic & Herb, Fresh Mushroom or Traditional sauce. Add whole cooked mushrooms and sliced olives. You can add 0% cholesterol Parmesan cheese to taste.
Total 300 calories and 3% fat based on 2oz spaghetti and ½ cup sauce

Salad with any Vinaigrette Dressing
Total 100 calories 7% fat

Garlic Bread with Home Churned Buttery Spread and Garlic powder to taste
Total 140 calories per slice and about 13% fat

Juice or Soda or Water at the high side the soda has the most calories which is around 160

## TOTAL CHOLESTEROL 0 % ZERO, ZIP, NADA & ABOUT 700 CAL

# SNACK

Oranges, Banana's, Apples, Peaches, Pears, Plums or any other fruit. Fresh is better but canned is OK if you want. Diced fruit cut.

Diced fruit approx. 125 calories per 1 ½ cut

## TOTAL CHOLESTEROL 0 %, ZERO, ZIP, NADA & MIN CALORIES

# BREAKFAST
## OATMEAL & CUT FRUIT

3 packs of Instant Oatmeal like Maple & Brown Sugar, Peaches & Cream, Regular or Apples & Cinnamon. Add sliced Fruit mix it up, more is good.
Oatmeal 100 to 160 each package depending on what flavor and about 50 calories for the sliced fruit. You can add juice if you like.

# LUNCH

Peanut Butter and Jelly sandwich any bread and any Jelly Preserve with juice and fruit.
Peanut butter 160 calories and 24% fat per 2 tablespoons.
2 slices of bread 140 calories and 2% fat
Preserve or Jelly 50 calories preserve 0% fat per 1 tablespoon.
100 calories 0% fat 8oz apple juice
1 piece of fruit has approx 50 calories 0% fat. Today we have orange slices and banana slices with chocolate syrup. Has about 100 calories per two tablespoons.

## TOTAL CHOLESTEROL 0%, ZERO, ZIP, NADA & AROUND 550 CAL.

# DINNER

## ASIAN STIR FRY

Broccoli, cauliflower, celery, mushroom, carrots, snow peas and any vegetables you like. Stir Fried in a deep pan skillet. Add Kikkoman Teriyaki Sauce. Heat on medium while stirring until vegetables are tended but crisp.

Calories approx. 250 depending on how many vegetables and Teriyaki you use. The veggies are about 20 calories per ½ cup and the Teriyaki sauce is 30 calories and 0% fat per one tablespoon.

Minute made ready to serve yellow rice. Cook in microwave for 60 seconds
220 calories 0% cholesterol 5% Fat per serving.

Total calories about 450 0% cholesterol 0% fat

## TOTAL CHOLESTEROL 0 % ZERO, ZIP, NADA & ABOUT 450 CAL

# BREAKFAST

Cheerios with sliced fruit
Cheerios has 100 calories per 1 cup have 2 or 3
Almond milk vanilla has 90 calories per 8 oz
The fruit has about 10 calories.

Total calories 400 based on 2 cups of Cheerios and 16 oz of Almond milk.

Total calories about 400 0% fat

## TOTAL CHOLESTEROL 0 % ZERO, ZIP, NADA & ABOUT 450 CAL

# LUNCH
## SALAD

Iceberg lettuce, Spinach, Portobello Mushrooms sauté in margarine, Tomatoes, Mandarin Oranges, Sprouts, Radish, Avocado, Cucumber, Baby Corn, Star Fruit, along with any other veggie you can think of then top it off with Croutons and Vinaigrette Dressing.

Salad has about 60 calories per 1 cup

Vinaigrette Dressing has about 60 calories and 7% fat per 2 tablespoons.

Total calories and fat based on 2 cup of salad and 4 tablespoons of dressing is about 240 calories and 14% fat.

## TOTAL CHOLESTEROL 0%, ZERO, ZIP, NADA & AROUND 240 CAL.

# DINNER
## SWEET & SOUR STIR FRY

Stir fried veggie on a bed of white rice with Sweet & Sour Glazing Sauce.

Fry Broccoli, cauliflower, celery, mushroom, carrots, snow peas, Bell peppers, bamboo shoots, onions, water chestnuts, yellow squash, zucchini, straw mushrooms and any vegetables you like. Stir Fried in a deep pan skillet with two table spoons of corn oil. Heat on medium while stirring until vegetables are tended but crisp. Cook white rice in a bag or instant. Then put the rice on a plate, put the veggies next. Topped with sprouts and Sweet & Sour Sauce. Garnish with baby corn.

Calories are approx. 150 depending on how many vegetables per ½ cup x 3 servings. Sweet & Sour sauce is 60 calories and 0% fat per one tablespoon. The rice is 140 calories per ½ cup. Add a drink and you have dinner.

Total calories about 300 0% fat

## TOTAL CHOLESTEROL 0 % ZERO, ZIP, NADA & ABOUT 300 CAL

# BREAKFAST

Kashi Go Lean with sliced fruit
Go Lean has 160 calories per 1 cup have
Almond milk vanilla has 90 calories per 8 oz
The fruit has about 10 calories.

Total calories 420 based on 2 cups of Go Lean and 8 oz of Almond milk.

Total calories about 420 2% fat

## TOTAL CHOLESTEROL 0 % ZERO, ZIP, NADA & ABOUT 420 CAL

# LUNCH

Bean Charras Tostados 5" Take two Tostados ¼ cup La Costena Refried Pinto Beans. Put lettuce, diced tomatoes, Imitation cheddar cheese and Pace Picante Sauce on top of beans use a lime or taco sauce to taste.

Tostados 0% Cholesterol 14% fat and 65 calories per tostado
Beans 0% Cholesterol 12% fat and approx. 35 calories per 2 table spoons
Diced tomatoes approx, 10 calories 0% cholesterol 0% fat
Save Today Imitation Cheddar Cheese 20 Calories 0% cholesterol 0% fat
Pace Picante Sauce 10 calories per 2 tablespoons 0% cholesterol 0% fat
Taco sauce 20 calories 0% cholesterol 0% fat per 2 tablespoons
Avocado 50 calories 0% cholesterol 15% fat base on 1/8 of a 6 oz avocado
Fruit approx 15 calories 0% cholesterol 0% fat
Dr Pepper Cherry 160 calories 0% cholesterol 0% fat per 12 oz can

Total calories about 350 26% fat based on two Tostados plus the Dr Pepper

## TOTAL CHOLESTEROL 0 % ZERO, ZIP, NADA & ABOUT 350 CAL

# DINNER
## PIZZA

Ready made pizza crust form 12" Mama Mary's topped with; Start with Pasta sauce with garlic and herb, it taste better then pizza sauce, Spread a layer on the crust sprinkle with garlic power and top with Portobello Mushrooms sauté in margarine, Tomatoes green & red, Sprouts, Radish, Avocado, Baby Corn, Olives, Broccoli, Cauliflower, Marinated Garlic cut in half, Marinated Artichoke Heart, onions, Mild Banana Peppers, Chives along with any other veggie you can think of then top it off with olive oil on curst. Cook in over about 8 to 9 minutes, let cool 2 minutes and top off with Shredded Imitation Mozzarella and Cheddar Cheese. Imitation cheese has 0% cholesterol.

Serving size is 1/6 of a pizza it has about 225 calories and 2% fat

Based on two slices total calories about 450 4% fat per serving

## TOTAL CHOLESTEROL 0 % ZERO, ZIP, NADA & ABOUT 450 CAL

14

# BREAKFAST

Apple Turn Over store bought not rocket science. With cut fruit
Total calories 180 and 15% fat per ½ turn over. I am sorry but I do not know anyone who eats ½ of a turn over. SO,

Based on 1 whole apple turn over total calories are 360 and fat is 30% with the cut fruit of 15 calories. Total calories are 195 and 15% fat. Plus a drink.

**TOTAL CHOLESTEROL 0 % ZERO, ZIP, NADA & ABOUT 375 CAL**

# LUNCH

Bean burrito take one 8" flour tortilla Spread ¼ cup refried beans on the tortilla and put it in the microwave for 10-15 seconds. Top with lettuce, diced tomatoes, imitation cheddar cheese, diced inions, 1/8 avocado cut into two slices and topped with Pace Picante Sauce add fruit and a Dr Pepper Cherry soda.

8" Flour tortilla 120 calories 0% cholesterol 4% fat

Lettuce approx 5 calories 0% cholesterol 0% fat

Imitation cheddar cheese 20 calories 0% cholesterol 3% fat base 1/8 cup

Diced tomatoes approx. 10 calories 0% cholesterol 0% fat

Pace Picante Sauce 10 calories 0% cholesterol 0% fat per 2 tablespoons

1/8 Avocado cut into 2 slices 50 calories 0% cholesterol 0% fat base on one medium 6 oz avocado

Fruit approx 5 calories 0% cholesterol 0% fat

Dr Pepper Cherry 160 calories 0% cholesterol 0% fat per 12 oz can

## TOTAL CHOLESTEROL 0 % ZERO, ZIP, NADA & ABOUT 375 CAL

# DINNER

## BBQ STYLE BURGER

1 Gardein Beefless Burger 130 calories 0% cholesterol 0% fat

1 Cobblestone Mill Onion Bun 160 calories 0% cholesterol 3% fat

BBQ sauce your choice 30 calories 0% cholesterol 0% fat per 2 tablespoon

Lettuce, Tomato slice and onion approx 10 calories 0% cholesterol 0% fat add a Dr Pepper

Cherry soda 160 calories 0% cholesterol 0% fat

Total calories 480 3% fat

## TOTAL CHOLESTEROL 0 % ZERO, ZIP, NADA & ABOUT 480 CAL

# BREAKFAST

English muffin with margarine, Strawberry Preserve and sliced fruit.
Calories muffin 120 fat 2%, Strawberry Preserve per 2 tablespoons 100 calories and 15 calories for the fruit Plus a drink.

Total calories 235 cholesterol 0% and fat 3%

## TOTAL CHOLESTEROL 0 % ZERO, ZIP, NADA & ABOUT 235 CAL

# LUNCH

Progresso Vegetable Classic Lentil Soup

Lentil soup with 5 Saltine Crackers
Lentil soup 320 calories 0% cholesterol 3% fat per 2 servings 1 can
Five saltine crackers 60 calories 0% cholesterol 2% fat

## TOTAL CHOLESTEROL 0 % ZERO, ZIP, NADA & ABOUT 280 CAL

# DINNER

## HICKORY BBQ RIBLETS

Morning Star Farms Hickory BBQ Riblet, Betty Crocker Roasted Garlic Mashed Potatoes, Peas in a can and cucumber slices.

BBQ Riblet 210 calories 0% cholesterol 5% fat
Roasted garlic mashed potatoes 80 calories 0% cholesterol 0% fat per 2/3 cup serving
Pea's 80 calories 0% cholesterol 0% fat per ½ cup serving
3 or 4 slices of cucumber about 1 teaspoon of Balsamic Vinaigrette dressing 7 calories 0% cholesterol 0% fat
Home Churned Buttery Spread 70 calories 0% cholesterol 12% fat
This is really, really good!!! Add a drink and your set.

Total 450 calories 0% cholesterol 17% fat

## TOTAL CHOLESTEROL 0 % ZERO, ZIP, NADA & ABOUT 450 CAL

# BREAKFAST

2 Blueberry Toaster Strudel with sliced fruit and Hershey's Chocolate Syrup
Cook in toaster until golden put sliced fruit on the side and top with Hershey's Chocolate zigzag lines
Blueberry strudel 170 calories 0% cholesterol 10% fat
Hershey's Chocolate Syrup 50 calories 0% cholesterol 0% fat per ½ tablespoon
Sliced fruit approx 10 calories 0% cholesterol 0% fat

Total calories is based on 2 strudel 1 tablespoon syrup

## TOTAL CHOLESTEROL 0% ZERO, ZIP, NADA & ABOUT 450 CAL

# LUNCH

## VEGETABLE ROTINI

4 oz of Tri-Color Rotini, 1 cup Broccoli cut into bite size pieces, ¾ cup Cauliflower cut into bite size pieces, about 12 large olives cut into half, about 12 cherry Tomatoes cut into half, 3 baby corn cut into quarters, 1 medium Avocado sliced this into 10 or 12 slices. Then mix with about 4-6 oz of Zesty Italian salad dressing.

4 oz Tri-Color Rotini 420 calories 0% cholesterol 2% fat
4 oz of Zesty Italian Salad Dressing 60 calories 0% cholesterol 0% fat
1 medium Avocado 300 calories 0% cholesterol 0% 15% fat
Baby Corn, Olives, Broccoli, Cauliflower, and Marinated Garlic approx.
100 calories 0% cholesterol 0% fat

Makes about 5 servings Total 880 calories 0% cholesterol 17% fat
0% cholesterol 6% fat 350 calories based on 2 cup serving

## TOTAL CHOLESTEROL 0% ZERO, ZIP, NADA & ABOUT 350 CAL

# DINNER

## GARDEIN BEFFLESS TIPS WITH RICE

Take one bag of Gardein Beefless Tips, cook in skillet with 2 tablespoons of BBQ sauce. Sautee 5 large sliced mushroom in Home Churned Buttery Spread. Steam sliced zucchini, squash, ¼ large onion and carrots. Put the rice on a plate topped with the sauté mushrooms and put the vegetables on the side. Add a soda This serves 4

Gardein Beefless Tips 325 calories 0% cholesterol 9% fat
Instant brown rice 150 calories 0% cholesterol 1% fat
Zucchini, carrots, squash & onion approx 100 calories 0% cholesterol 0% fat
Home Churned Buttery Spread. 70 calories 0% cholesterol 12% fat
Soda 160 calories 0% cholesterol 0% fat per 12 oz can

Total approx 300 calories 0% cholesterol 13% fat per serving

# CHAPTER TWO

*This chapter is devoted to meals that have less then 12% cholesterol each with a total intake of less then 36% or less each day.*

*Naturally less cholesterol is better, but most of the really good tasting meals have some cholesterol. The trick is to keep the cholesterol down to a minimum.*

*Close to zero is good*

*For those of you who really do not like cooking. We have come up with some of the better meals that are pre-made (frozen)*

# THE CHOLESTEROL LESS THEN 12% PER MEALS

# BREAKFAST

## EGGS PLUS

Coburn farm eggzactly equal to 2 eggs with pancakes, sausage and hash browns. Cut fresh fruit

Eggzactlt 60 calories 0% cholesterol 0% fat

2 Morning Star sausages links 50 calories 0% cholesterol 0% fat

3 Frozen med. Pancakes with one tablespoon Morning Delight Syrup

350 calories 5% cholesterol 8% fat

Hash Browns 80 calories 0% cholesterol 0% fat

Cut fresh fruit 15 calories 0% cholesterol 0% fat

Total 545 calories 5% cholesterol 8% fat

# LUNCH
## PRE-MADE

Lightlife Frozen Dinner, Pene Primavera with meatless crumbles. Lettuce, sliced cucumber and cherry tomatoes. Add a cherry coke.

Primavera with meatless crumbles 240 calories 2% cholesterol 7% fat
Salad with Kraft Zesty Italian dressing 15 calories 0% cholesterol 0% fat per 2 tablespoons
Cherry coke 160 calories 0% cholesterol 0% fat

Total 415 calories 2% cholesterol 7% fat

# DINNER

## LEAN CUISINE

Lean Cuisine Spaghetti with meat sauce. Lettuce, sliced cucumber and cherry tomatoes salad. Add a Cherry Dr Pepper, can you tell I like Cherry Dr Pepper?

Lean Cuisine Spaghetti 320 calories 3% cholesterol 6% fat
Salad with Kraft Zesty Italian dressing 15 calories 0% cholesterol 0% fat
per 2 tablespoons
Cherry coke 160 calories 0% cholesterol 0% fat

Total 495 calories 3% cholesterol 6% fat

**TOTAL FOR THE DAY 1455 calories 10% cholesterol 21% fat**

# BREAKFAST
## TOASTER STRUDEL

Toaster Strudel with fresh fruit

Two Toaster Strudels 340 calories 0% cholesterol 20% fat
Fresh cot fruit approx 10 calories 0% cholesterol 0% fat

Total 350 calories 0% cholesterol 20% fat

# LUNCH

## PEA SOUP

Progresso Split Pea Soup with saltine crackers

Progresso Split Pea Soup 320 calories 1% cholesterol 4% fat
5 Saltine Crackers 60 calories 0% cholesterol 2% fat

Total 360 calories 1% cholesterol 6% fat

# DINNER

## PULLED BEEF

Curly's BBQ Pulled Beef with Bush's Beans

Curly's BBQ Pulled Beef 60 calories 5% cholesterol 3% fat per ¼ cup
Cobblestone Mill Onion Rolls (bun) 180 calories 0% cholesterol 3% fat
Bush's Bean with onions and Imitation cheddar cheese 150 calories 0% cholesterol 2% fat
with cheese and onions

Total 390 calories 5% cholesterol 8% fat

**TOTAL FOR THE DAY 1100 calories 4% cholesterol 34% fat**

# BREAKFAST

Apple Turn Over store bought not rocket science. With cut fruit
Total calories 180 and 15% fat per ½ turn over. I am sorry but I do not know anyone who eats ½ of a turn over. SO, here we go again

Based on 1 whole apple turn over total calories are 360 and fat is 30% with the cut fruit of 15 calories. Total calories are 195 and 15% fat. Plus a drink.
Florida's Natural Orange Juice as much as you want
110 calories 0% cholesterol 0% fat per 8oz glass

Total 485 calories 0% cholesterol 30% fat

## TOTAL CHOLESTEROL 0 % ZERO, ZIP, NADA & ABOUT 485 CAL

# LUNCH
## BLT WITH POTATO SALAD

Turkey Bacon with tomato, lettuce and whipped salad dressing on toast
Add potato salad and cut fresh fruit

Turkey bacon 60 calories 6% cholesterol 8% fat per 2 slices
Toast 140 calories 1% cholesterol 0% fat per 2 slices
Whipped dressing 60 calories 1% cholesterol 5% fat
Lettuce and tomato 25 calories 0% cholesterol 0% fat
Fresh fruit approx 30 calories 0% cholesterol 0% fat
Potato salad 160 calories 4% cholesterol 20% fat

Total 415 calories 12% cholesterol 33% fat

# DINNER

# FISH & CHIPS

Beer Battered Fish Fillets with French Fries and a Salad

Beer Battered Fish Fillet 270 calories 6% cholesterol 11% fat per 1 fish fillet
French Fries 150 calories 2% cholesterol 11% fat deep fried per 3 oz
Salad approx 30 calories 0% cholesterol 0% fat
Tarter Sauce 70 calories 1% cholesterol 9% fat
Salad Dressing 60 calories 0% cholesterol 6% fat per 2 tablespoon

Total 580 calories 9% cholesterol 37% fat

**TOTAL FOR THE DAY 1480 calories 21% cholesterol 100% fat**

# BREAKFAST
## EGGS, WAFFLE & SAUSAGE

Coburn farm eggzactly equal to 2 eggs, waffle, sausage and hash browns. Cut fresh fruit

Eggzactlt 60 calories 0% cholesterol 0% fat equal per 2 egg
2 Morning Star sausages links 50 calories 0% cholesterol 0% fat
2 Frozen med. Waffle with one tablespoon Morning Delight Syrup
310 calories 4% cholesterol 14% fat
Cut fresh fruit 5 calories 0% cholesterol 0% fat

Total 365 4% cholesterol 14% fat

# LUNCH
## SMOKED SAUSAGE

Smoked Sausage on a bed of Sauerkraut a salad and drink

Smoked Sausage 180 calories 10% cholesterol 25% fat per 2 oz
Sauerkraut 5 calories 0% fat per 1 oz
Salad with Ranch dressing approx 80 calories 1% fat

Total 265 11% cholesterol 26% fat

# DINNER
## ORIENTAL STIR FRY

Broccoli, cauliflower, celery, mushroom, carrots, snow peas, snap peas, water chestnuts, bamboo, sprouts, olives, cut into half marinated garlic, zucchini, squash plus you can add any vegetables you like. Stir Fried in a deep pan skillet. Heat on medium while stirring until vegetables are tended but crisp. Steam the asparagus and put on the side. Then cook chicken cut into 1" squares and add to veggies. Add La Choy Sweet & Sour Sauce when finished cooking.

Calories approx. 250 depending on how many vegetables and Sweet & Sour Sauce you use. The veggies are about 30 calories per ½ cup and the Sweet & Sour Sauce is 60 calories 0% cholesterol 0% fat per one tablespoon.

Chicken is approx. 120 calories 8% cholesterol 5% fat per 3 oz

Total 400 calories 8% cholesterol 5% fat

**TOTAL FOR THE DAY 1030 calories 19% cholesterol 45% fat**

# BREAKFAST
## CREERIOS & STRAWBERRIES

Cheerios with Strawberries and
Cheerios has 100 calories per 1 cup have 2 or 3
Almond milk vanilla has 90 calories per 8 oz
The strawberries have about 10 calories.

Total calories 400 based on 2 cups of Cheerios and 16 oz of Almond milk.
Florida's Natural Orange Juice 110 calories 0% cholesterol 0% fat per 8oz glass
Strawberries 10 calories 0% cholesterol 0% fat

Total calories about 400 0% cholesterol 0% fat

## TOTAL CHOLESTEROL 0 % ZERO, ZIP, NADA & ABOUT 450 CAL

# LUNCH

## TURKEY SANDWICH

Turkey sandwich with lettuce, tomato and Salad Dressing with Sautee mushrooms and asparagus on the side, add Welch's 100% Grape Juice

Turkey 50 calories 8% cholesterol 2% fat per 2 oz
White breads 70 calories 0% cholesterol 0% fat per 1 slice
Whipped Dressing 60 calories 0% cholesterol 0% fat per 1 tablespoon
Lettuce and tomato approx 10 calories 0% cholesterol 0% fat
Sautee mushrooms and asparagus approx 45 calories 0% cholesterol 0% fat
Welch's 100% Grape Juice 150 calories 0% cholesterol 0% fat per 8 oz

Total 455 8% cholesterol 2% fat

# DINNER

## HAWAIIAN STIR FRY

Chicken strips cut into 1-2" squares cook in separate pan. Broccoli, mushroom, carrots, pineapple chunks (approx 6 cups) stir fried in a deep pan skillet. Asparagus is sauté on the side in a separate pan. Add about 4 Tablespoons each of Lawry's Hawaiian Sauce and Thai Sweet Chili Sauce. Then heat on medium while stirring until vegetables are tended but crisp. Makes approx 4 servings

Chicken 120 calories 10% cholesterol 5% fat per 3 oz
Lawry's Hawaiian Sauce 80 calories 0% cholesterol 0% fat per 4 tablespoon
Thai Sweet Chili Sauce 40 calories 0% cholesterol 0% fat per 4 tablespoons
Vegetables Broccoli, mushrooms, carrots, pineapple, asparagus is approx.
100 calories 0% cholesterol 0% fat

Kiwi, cantaloupe, honeydew and strawberry 25 calories 0% cholesterol 0% fat
Total 365 calories 10% cholesterol 5% fat per serving

**TOTAL FOR THE DAY 1220 calories 18% cholesterol 7% fat**

# BREAKFAST

## BLUEBERRY OATMEAL

3 packs of Instant Oatmeal like Maple & Brown Sugar, Peaches & Cream, Regular, Apples & Cinnamon of Blueberry. Add sliced Fruit mix it up, more is good.

Oatmeal 100 to 160 each package depending on what flavor and about 20 calories for the sliced fruit. You can add juice if you like.

Oat Meal 320 calories 0% cholesterol 0% fat

# LUNCH

## CHEESE ENCHILADA

El Charrito Queso Enchilada Dinner with rice & beans. Cook as directed add Pace Chunky Salsa plus a Cherry Dr Pepper

Cheese Enchilada Rice & beans 340 calories 3% cholesterol 11% fat
Cherry Dr Pepper 160 calories 0% cholesterol 0% fat
Pace Salsa 10 calories 0% cholesterol 0% fat per 2 tablespoons

Total 510 calories 3% cholesterol 11% fat

# DINNER
## ASIAN BEEF & BROCCOLI

Asian Beef and Broccoli on a bed of Brown Rice with a Savory Soy Garlic Sauce

Beef and broccoli with soy garlic sauce 250 calories 7% cholesterol 11% fat per 1 cup serving
Brown rice instant 150 calories 0% cholesterol 1% fat per ½ cup serving

Total 400 calories 7% cholesterol l2% fat [per serving

**TOTAL FOR THE DAY calories 1230 10% cholesterol 23% fat**

# BREAKFAST

## FRENCH TOAST

Winn Dixie French Toast Morning Delight Syrup fresh cut fruit and Florida Natural Orange Juice

5 French toast sticks 320 calories 7% cholesterol 25% fat
Morning Delight Syrup 200 calories 0% cholesterol 0% fat per ¼ cup
Florida Natural Orange Juice 110 calories 0% cholesterol 0% fat per 8 oz
Fresh cut Fruit approx 50 calories 0% cholesterol 0% fat

Total 680 calories 7% cholesterol 25% fat

# LUNCH
## MANICOTTI

Michelina's Cheese Manicotti with marinated garlic cloves. cut tomatoes, garlic bread and sprinkled with parmesan cheese, Plus a drink

Michelina's Cheese Manicotti dinner (frozen) 230 calories 5% cholesterol 12% fat
Garlic Bread about 100 calories 0% cholesterol 12% fat
Parmesan Cheese 10 calories 1% cholesterol 2% fat per 1teaspoon
One sliced tomato about 20 calories 0% cholesterol 0% fat
Marinated Garlic Cloves 10 calories 0% cholesterol 0% fat

Total 370 calories 6% cholesterol 19% fat

# DINNER
## LASAGNA

Smart Ones Lasagna Florentine with Garlic Bread and Marinated Garlic Cloves Plus a drink

Smart Ones Lasagna Florentine Dinner (frozen) calories 320 6% cholesterol 16% fat
Garlic Bread about 100 calories 0% cholesterol 12% fat
Parmesan Cheese 10 calories 1% cholesterol 2% fat per 1teaspoon
Marinated Garlic Cloves 10 calories 0% cholesterol 0% fat

Total 430 calories 7% cholesterol 30% fat

**TOTAL FOR THE DAY calories 1480 30% cholesterol 74% fat**

# CHAPTER THREE

*This chapter is devoted to meals that have less then 13% cholesterol each with a total intake of less then 39% or less each day.*

## THE CHOLESTEROL LESS THEN 13% PER MEALS

# BREAKFAST
## SIMPLE

Cinnamon Roll with Fresh Fruit

Cinnamon Roll 240 calories 2% cholesterol 9% fat
Fresh Fruit 20 calories 0% cholesterol 0% fat

Total 240 calories 2% cholesterol 9% fat

# LUNCH

## JAMAICAN STYLE BURGER

Gardein beefless burger on onion bun with lettuce, tomato, onion and pickle topped off with Jamaican Jerk Sauce and one medium potato sliced into French fries and deep fried to a golden brown

Onion bun 180 calories 0% cholesterol 3% fat
Beefless burger 130 calories 0% cholesterol 3% fat
French fries 150 calories 2% cholesterol 8 % fat
Jerk sauce 25 calories 0% cholesterol 0% fat
Garnish 25 calories 0% cholesterol 0%fat

Total 510 calories 2% cholesterol 14% fat

# DINNER
## CHICKEN VEGETABLES

Lean Cuisine Roasted Chicken and Garden Vegetables with pasta and Garlic Mashed Potatoes

Lean Cuisine Roasted Chicken and Garden Vegetables 230 calories 8% cholesterol 5% fat
Roasted Garlic Mashed Potatoes 100 calories 0% cholesterol 0% fat
Two slices of Kiwi fruit 0% cholesterol 0% fat

Total 330 calories 8% cholesterol 5% fat

**TOTAL FOR THE DAY 1080 calories 12% cholesterol 28% fat**

# BREAKFAST
## SIMPLE

Shredded Wheat with Almond Milk topped with fresh fruit and Florida's Natural Orange Juice

Shredded Wheat 180 calories 0% cholesterol 2 % fat per two biscuits
Almond milk vanilla has 90 calories 0 % cholesterol 0% fat per 8 oz
Fresh Fruit approx 20 calories 0% cholesterol 0% fat
Florida's Natural Orange Juice 110 calories 0% cholesterol 0% fat

Total 400 calories 0% cholesterol 2% fat

# LUNCH

## MANWICH

Hunts Manwich Sloppy Joe (pre-made) on an onion bun with Tropical fruit salad (in a can)

Hunts Manwich Sloppy Joe 70 calories 2% cholesterol 5% fat per 3 tablespoons
Onion bun 160 calories 0 cholesterol 3%fat
Fruit Salad 100 calories 0% cholesterol 0% fat

Total 330 calories 2% cholesterol 8% fat

# DINNER
## STOUFFERS BEEF POT ROAST

Stouffers Beef Pot Roast Frozen Dinner add Garlic Mashed Potatoes and you have dinner

Stouffers Beef Pot Roast 210 calories 8% cholesterol 6% fat
Betty Crocker instant Mashed Potatoes 100 calories 0% cholesterol 0% fat do not add milk use all water to cook

Total 310 calories 8% cholesterol 6% fat

**TOTAL FOR THE DAY 1040 calories 10% cholesterol 16% fat**

# BREAKFAST

Toasted Wheat Chex with Fresh Fruit and Almond Milk and Florida's Natural Orange Juice

Wheat Chex 160 calories 0% cholesterol 1% fat

Fresh Fruit approx 50 calories 0% cholesterol 0% aft

Almond Milk 90 calories 0% cholesterol 0% fat

Florida's Natural Orange Juice 110 calories 0% cholesterol 0% fat

Total 410 calories 0% cholesterol 1% fat

# LUNCH
## VEGGIE WRAP

One 8" Tortilla with Broccoli, Cauliflower, snap peas, diced onions, zucchini, olives, garlic cloves and carrots all cut into small pieces stir fried and rolled up in a flour tortilla and a Cherry Dr Pepper and you have lunch
Kiwi Fruit as a garnish

One 8" tortilla 180 calories 0% cholesterol 8% fat
Stir fried vegetables approx 120 calories 0% cholesterol 0% fat before cooking
Cherry Dr Pepper 160 calories 0% cholesterol 0% fat

Total 460 calories 0% cholesterol 8% fat

# DINNER

## SAUSAGE PIZZA

Sausage and Vegetable Pizza with sliced sausage, mushrooms, onions, tomatoes and garlic cloves all diced and sliced. Spaghetti sauce instead of pizza sauce because it taste better. 1/3 cup of pizza cheese, cook for 10-12 minutes at 425

Mama Mary's Pizza Crust per one slice 180 calories 0% cholesterol 8% fat

Smoke Sausage 30 calories 5% cholesterol 6% fat per two slices (average 2 slices of sausage per slice of pizza) approx 12-14 slices of sausage per pizza

2/3 cup of pizza cheese total per pizza approx per slice of pizza 40 calories 4% cholesterol 5% fat

Mushrooms, onion, tomatoes and sliced garlic cloves 80 calories 0% cholesterol 0%fat

Pizza Sauce 25 calories 0% cholesterol 0% fat per ¼ cup but use ½ cup

Cherry Dr Pepper 160 calories 0% cholesterol 0%fat

Total 515 calories 9% cholesterol 19% fat

**TOTAL FOR THE DAY 1385 calories 9% cholesterol 28% fat**

# BREAKFAST
## OPEN FACE CHEESE OMELETTE

Coburn Farm Eggzactly approx 2 eggs cooked open face with diced tomatoes, onions and mushrooms sprinkle with cheese after it is cooked plus Turkey Bacon and Fresh Fruit on the side

Coburn Farm Eggzactly approx 2 eggs approx 100 calories 0% cholesterol 0% fat
Shredded Imitation Mozzarella and/or Cheddar Cheese 90 calories 0% cholesterol 9% fat per ½ cup
Turkey Bacon 60 calories 6% cholesterol 4% fat per 2 slices
Fresh Fruit approx 40 calories 0% cholesterol 0% fat
Florida's Natural Orange Juice 110 calories 0% cholesterol 0% fat

Total 400 calories 6% cholesterol 13% fat

# LUNCH

## FRIED CLAMS

Mrs. Paul's Fried Clams with Winn Dixie Old Fashioned Potato Salad. Add lemon slices, Tarter Sauce and a Cheery Dr Pepper, Lunch is served.

Mrs. Paul's Fried Clams 270 calories 7% cholesterol 20% fat
Potato Salad 270 calories 5% cholesterol 28% fat
Cherry Dr Pepper 160 calories 0% cholesterol 0% fat

Total 700 calories 12% cholesterol 48% fat

# DINNER
## PASTA AND SAUSAGE

Penne Pasta with Sausage with diced tomatoes, onions, mushroom and marinated garlic cloves topped with pasta sauce add a drink and you're done

Penne Pasta approx 210 calories 0% cholesterol 2% fat per two cups
Smoked Sausage 150 calories 8% cholesterol 10% fat per 2oz sliced
Pasta Sauce 160 calories 0% cholesterol 8% fat per one cup
One Dr Pepper 160 calories 0% cholesterol 0% fat

Total 470 calories 8% cholesterol 20% fat

**TOTAL FOR THE DAY 1570 calories 26% cholesterol 81% fat**

# BREAKFAST
## REAL CHEESE OMLETTE PLUS

Coburn Farm Eggzactly omelet with diced mushrooms, olives, onion and tomatoes plus pancakes and fresh berries with syrup and turkey bacon. Add a glass of Florida's Natural Orange Juice.

Coburn Farm Eggzactly 90 calories 0% cholesterol 0% fat per three eggs

Mushrooms, olives, onions and tomatoes approx. 50 calories 0% chol 0% fat

Real cheese 90 calories 7% cholesterol 11% fat per ¼ cup

Turkey Bacon 60 calories 6% cholesterol 8% fat per two strips

Pancakes 300 calories 0% cholesterol 0% fat

Syrup 200 calories 0% cholesterol 0% fat

Fresh Berries approx. 15 calories 0% cholesterol 0% fat

Florida's Natural Orange Juice 110 calories 0% cholesterol 0% fat

Total 915 calories 13% cholesterol 19% fat

# LUNCH
## HOT DOG

Oscar Mayer Extra Lean Franks 95% fat free made with Turkey. Winn Dixie Red Skin Potato Salad and one cup of cut Fruit

Oscar Mayer Frank 90 calories 7% cholesterol 4% fat per hot dog
Hot Dog Bun 110 calories 0% cholesterol 0% fat per one bun
Potato Salad 260 calories 5% cholesterol 28% fat
Cut Fruit Salad approx 100 calories 0% cholesterol 0% fat per one cup

Total 560 calories 12% cholesterol 34% fat

# DINNER
## GENERAL TSO'S CHICKEN

Kahiki General Tso's Chicken with Kahiki Chicken Egg Rolls with Sweet & Sour Sauce (frozen dinner) Serving per Container 4 each

Kahiki General Tso's Chicken 320 calories 3% cholesterol 11% fat per 1 cup serving per Container 4 Serving

Kahiki Chicken Egg Rolls with Sweet & Sour Sauce 140 calories 2% cholesterol 4% fat serving per Container 4 Serving size 1 egg roll

Total 460 calories 5% cholesterol 15% fat

**TOTAL FOR THE DAY 1935 calories 30% cholesterol 68% fat**

# BREAKFAST

Frosted Mini Wheat with Whole Milk and Fresh Cut Strawberries

Frosted Mini Wheat 190 calories 0% cholesterol 2% fat per one cup
Whole Milk 150 calories 11% cholesterol 12% fat per one cup
Two diced strawberries <5 calories 0% cholesterol 0% fat

Total 340 calories 11% cholesterol 12% fat

# LUNCH
## TURKEY SAUSAGE KEBABS

California Style Turkey Sausage Kebabs with Mushrooms, Bell Peppers, Cherry Tomatoes Zucchini and Onions and on the side sliced Avocados, Cucumbers and Cherry Tomatoes with Kraft Zesty Italian Dressing.

Turkey Sausage Kebabs 100 calories 11% cholesterol 8% fat per 2 oz
Mushrooms, Bell Peppers, Onions (not shown), Cherry Tomatoes Approx. 50 calories 0% cholesterol 0% fat
One half sliced Avocado 150 calories 0% cholesterol 1% fat
Sliced Cucumbers approx. 5 calories 0% cholesterol 0% fat
Kraft Zesty Italian Dressing 15 calories 0% chol 1% fat per 2 table spoons

Total 320 calories 11% cholesterol 10% fat

# DINNER
## SALMON & RICE

Gorton's Simply Bake Salmon with Roasted Garlic & Butter and a bed of Long Grain Wild Rice with Herb Seasoning each has two servings add a slice of lemon

Gorton's Simply Bake Salmon with Roasted Garlic & Butter 140 calories 7% cholesterol 4% fat serving size 1 piece
Long Grain Wild Rice with Herb Seasoning 160 calories 0% cholesterol 3% fat per 1 cup

Total 300 cholesterol 7% cholesterol 7% fat

**TOTAL FOR THE DAY 960 calories 29% cholesterol 29% fat**

# BREAKFAST

Strawberry Toaster Strudel with Vanilla and Chocolate syrup sliced Strawberries

Two Toaster Strudel's 340 calories 0% cholesterol 10% fat
Hershey's Double Chocolate Syrup 50 calories 0% cholesterol 0% fat per one tablespoon
Sliced Strawberries approx < 5 calories 0% cholesterol 0% fat

Total 400 calories 0% cholesterol 0% fat

# LUNCH
## BEEF TAQUITOS

Five Beef Taquitos with Rice and Refried Beans, Sliced Avocado and Cut Fresh Fruit

Five Tequitos 380 calories 5% cholesterol 23% fat

La Costena Refried Beans 140 calories 0% cholesterol 12 % fat per ½ cup

Uncle Ben's Country Inn Broccoli Rice Au Gratin w/o butter 200 calories 2% cholesterol 4% fat

Pace Chunky Salsa 10 calories 0% cholesterol 0% fat per 2 tablespoons

Cut Fresh Fruit 5 calories 0% cholesterol 0% fat

Total 735 calories 7% cholesterol 39% fat

# DINNER
## STEAK TIPS

Lean Cuisine Steak Tips Portobello with mushrooms in a savory beef sauce Broccoli and Betty Crocker's Roasted Garlic Mashed Potatoes on the side.

Lean Cuisine Steak Tips and Broccoli 150 calories 5% cholesterol 6% fat
Betty Crocker's Roasted Garlic Mashed Potatoes 80 calories 0% cholesterol 0% fat per 2/3 cup

Total 230 calories 5% cholesterol 6% fat

**TOTAL FOR THE DAY 1365 calories 45% cholesterol 68% fat**

# CHAPTER FOUR

*This chapter is devoted to meals that have less then 15% cholesterol each with a total intake of less then 45% or less each day.*

## THE CHOLESTEROL LESS THEN 15% PER MEALS

# BREAKFAST

## FRENCH TOAST

Coburn Farms EggZactly about ¼ cup Bread, Hash Browns and Syrup topped with freshly sliced strawberries

Coburn Farms EggZactly 90 calories 0% cholesterol 0% fat per 3 eggs equal
3 Slices of Bread 210 calories 0% cholesterol 0% fat
3 oz Hash Browns 80 calories 0% cholesterol 0% fat
Syrup 2 tablespoons 200 calories 0% cholesterol 0% fat
Sliced Strawberries 10 calories 0% cholesterol 0% fat

590 calories 0% cholesterol 0% fat

# LUNCH

## ROAST BEEF SANDWICH

Roast Beef Sandwich with Homemade French Fries

Roast Beef 80 calories 8% cholesterol 4% fat per 3 oz
Whipped Dressing 60 calories 1% cholesterol 5% fat
½ Large Potato cut thin 70 calories 0% cholesterol 0% fat
Two slices of Bread 140 calories 0% cholesterol 2% fat
Lettuce, Tomato approx 5 calories 0% cholesterol 0% fat

Total 355 calories 9% cholesterol 11% fat

# DINNER

## BAKED SALMON

Baked Salmon with steamed mixed vegetables and sliced lemons

Salmon 150 calories 15% cholesterol 2% fat per 4 oz
Steamed mixed vegetables 70 calories 0% cholesterol 0% fat

Total 220 calories 15% cholesterol 2% fat

**TOTAL FOR THE DAY 1165 calories 24% cholesterol 13% fat**

# BREAKFAST
## FRESH SLICED FRUIT

Sliced Avocado, Berries and fruit on a bed of lettuce

Sliced Avocado 150 calories 0% cholesterol 0% fat
Fresh Sliced Kiwi 50 calories 0% cholesterol 0% fat
Blueberries, Blackberries and Strawberries approx 30 calories 0% cholesterol 0% fat
Lettuce approx 5 calories 0% cholesterol 0% fat

Total 235 calories 0% cholesterol 0% fat

# LUNCH
## SOUP

Progresso Vegetable Classic Minestrone Soup with Saltine Crackers

Progresso Vegetable Minestrone Soup 200 calories 0% cholesterol 0% fat
Per one 19 oz can
Saltine Crackers 60 calories 0% cholesterol 2% fat per 5 crackers

Total 260 calories 0% cholesterol 2% fat

# DINNER
## GRILLED CHICKEN

Grilled Chicken with Roasted Garlic Mashed Potatoes covered with Sautee Sliced Portabella Mushrooms and Asparagus

Grilled chicken 120 calories 12% cholesterol 5% fat per 4 oz
Portabella Mushrooms 50 calories 0% cholesterol 0% fat per 2 medium Mushrooms
Roasted Garlic Mashed Potatoes 80 calories 0% cholesterol 0% fat using only water to mix
Asparagus approx 25 calories 0% cholesterol 0% fat

Total 275 calories 12% cholesterol 5% fat

**TOTAL FOR THE DAY 770 calories 12% cholesterol 7% fat**

# BREAKFAST

Raspberry Danish Breakfast Roll with Sliced Fresh Fruit

Raspberry Roll 210 calories 2% cholesterol 5% fat
Sliced Fresh Fruit approx 10 calories 0% cholesterol 0% fat

Total 220 calories 2% cholesterol 5% fat

# LUNCH

## RAVIOLI

Lean Cuisine Cheese Ravioli with Garlic Bread and Salad

Lean Cuisine Cheese Ravioli 250 calories 10% cholesterol 8% fat
Gruiseppe's Garlic Bread 200 calories 0% cholesterol 15% fat per 1/5 loaf
Small Dinner Salad approx 50 calories 0% cholesterol 0% fat
Kraft Zesty Italian dressing 15 calories 0% cholesterol 0% fat per 2 Tablespoons

Total 515 calories 0% cholesterol 15% fat

# DINNER

## CHICKEN ALFREDO

Lean Cuisine Alfredo Pasta with Chicken and Broccoli, Garlic Bread and on the side a Small Dinner Salad

Alfredo Pasta with Chicken and Broccoli 270 calories 10% cholesterol 6% fat
Garlic Bread 70 calories 0% cholesterol 0% fat
Home Churned Buttery Spread 70 calories 0% cholesterol 12% fat
Garlic Powder 5 calories 0% cholesterol 0% fat per ¼ Tablespoon
Small Dinner Salad 50 calories 0% cholesterol 0% fat
Kraft Zesty Italian dressing 15 calories 0% cholesterol 0% fat

Total 410 calories 10% cholesterol 18% fat

**TOTAL FOR THE DAY 1445 calories 12% cholesterol 40% fat**

# BREAKFAST

Blueberry Turnover with sliced fruit and Florida's Natural Orange Juice

Blueberry turnover 360 calories 0% cholesterol 15% fat
Sliced Fruit approx 80 calories 0% cholesterol 0% fat per 1 cup
Florida's Natural Orange Juice 100 calories 0% cholesterol 0% fat per 8 oz

Total 540 calories 0% cholesterol 15% fat

# LUNCH
## ZITI

Smart Ones Three Cheese Ziti Marinara with Garlic Bread and Cherry Doctor Pepper garnish with one Strawberry

Smart Ones Three Cheese Ziti Marinara 300 calories 4% cholesterol 13% fat
Garlic Bread 150 calories 0% cholesterol 13% fat per two 3" slices
Cherry Doctor Pepper 160 calories 0% cholesterol 0% fat

Total 610 calories 4% cholesterol 26% fat

# DINNER
## SPAGHETTI & MEATBALLS

Marie Callender's Spaghetti & Meatballs in a Hearty Marinara Sauce with Garlic Bread, Small Dinner Salad and garnished with an Onion

Marie Callender's Spaghetti & Meatballs 420 calories 12% cholesterol 20% fat
Garlic Bread 150 calories 0% cholesterol 13% fat per two 3" slices
Small Dinner Salad approx 50 calories 0% cholesterol 0% fat
Kraft Zesty Italian dressing 15 calories 0% cholesterol 0% fat per 2 Tablespoons
Cherry Doctor Pepper 160 calories 0% cholesterol 0% fat
Onion 5 Calories 0% cholesterol 0% fat

Total 800 calories 25% cholesterol 33% fat

## TOTAL FOR THE DAY 1950 calories 29% cholesterol 74% fat

# BREAKFAST
## SLICED FRUIT

One Wine Glass filled with Cut and Sliced Fresh Fruit topped with Whipped Cream

1 ½ to 2 cups of fresh cut and slices fruit and melons approx 75 calories 0% cholesterol 0% fat per 1 cup

Whipped Cream (Redi-whipped) in a can 15 calories 1% cholesterol 2% fat per 2 Tablespoons

Total 95 calories 1% cholesterol 2% fat

# LUNCH

Signature Sliders Chicken Sandwich with Progresso Clam Chowder Soup

Signature Chicken Sliders 270 calories 5% cholesterol 7% fat
Whipped Dressing 60 calories 1% cholesterol 7% fat
Lettuce and Tomatoes 5 calories 0% cholesterol 0% fat
Progresso Calm Chowder Soup 200 calories 1% cholesterol 3% fat per 19oz can

Total 535 calories 7% cholesterol 17% fat

# DINNER

Boneless Rib shape patties (per-made frozen) with BBQ Sauce add Betty Crocker Roasted Garlic Mash Potatoes and Sweet Peas topped of with a Doctor Pepper and an onion garnish

Boneless Rib Shaped Patties with BBQ Sauce 205 calories 8% cholesterol 15% fat
Betty Crocker Roasted Garlic Mashed Potatoes 80 calories 0% cholesterol 0% fat (Do not use milk to made) use water only to made per 2/3 cup
Sweet Peas 80 calories 0% cholesterol 0% fat per ½ cup
One onion garnish 5 calories 0% cholesterol 0% fat

Total 370 calories 8% cholesterol 15% fat

**TOTAL FOR THE DAY 1000 calories 16% cholesterol 34% fat**

# BREAKFAST
## EGG & VEGGIE WRAP

Coburn Farms EggZactly Eggs with Tomatoes, onions and Sautee all wrapped up in a flour Tortilla topped with Pace Salsa

Coburn Farms EggZactly 90 calories 0% cholesterol 0% fat per 3 eggs equal
Tomatoes, Onions and Mushrooms 25 calories 0% cholesterol 0% fat
10" Flour Tortilla 180 calories 0% cholesterol 8% fat
Pace Salsa 10 calories 0% cholesterol 0% fat per 2 Tablespoons

Total 305 calories 0% cholesterol 8% fat

# LUNCH

## CALIFORNIA SOFT TACO

California Soft Taco with Hamburger, Sliced Avocado, Lettuce, Tomatoes and Imitation Shredded Cheddar Cheese top with Pace Picante Sauce with a side of Pinto Beans

8" Flour Tortilla 130 calories 0% cholesterol 5% fat
Hamburger 93% lean 85 calories 11% cholesterol 6% fat per 2oz
Sliced Avocado approx 1/3 avocado 120 calories 0% cholesterol 0% fat
Pace Picante Sauce 10 calories 0% cholesterol 0% fat per 2 Tablespoons
Imitation Shredded Cheese 40 calories 0% cholesterol 0% fat
Lettuce and Tomatoes and Strawberries on the side approx 15 calories 0% cholesterol 0% fat
Pinto Beans 100 calories 0% cholesterol 2% fat per ½ cup

Total 500 calories 11% cholesterol 13% fat

# DINNER
## BAKED SALMON

Baked Skinless Pink Salmon with steamed Asparagus, Snow Peas, Broccoli and Sautee Mushrooms all on a bed of Zatarain's Wild Brown Rice add some sliced lemons and a Doctor Pepper and you have Dinner

Salmon 150 calories 15% cholesterol 2% fat per 4 oz
Steamed mixed vegetable 70 calories 0% cholesterol 0% fat
Zatarain's Wild Brown Rice 200 calories 0% cholesterol 2% fat
Doctor Pepper 160 calories 0% cholesterol 0% fat

Total 580 calories 15% cholesterol 4% fat

**TOTAL FOR THE DAY 1385 calories 26% cholesterol 25% fat**

# BREAKFAST

Strawberry Toaster Strudel with Strawberry Preserves, Sliced Kiwi and Strawberries topped with Hershey's Double Chocolate Syrup

Two Toaster Strudels 340 calories 0% cholesterol 10% fat
Hershey's Double Chocolate Syrup 50 calories 0% cholesterol 0% fat per one tablespoon
Sliced Strawberries and Kiwi approx 10 calories 0% cholesterol 0% fat

Total 400 calories 0% cholesterol 0% fat

# LUNCH
## CALIFORNIA HAMBURGER

California Meatless Hamburger on Sour Dough Bread, lettuce, tomatoes and onion with Garlic Shell & Cheese topped off with sliced fresh fruit. Add a Doctor Pepper and you got a California lunch.

1 Gardein Beefless Burger 130 calories 0% cholesterol 0% fat
Lettuce, Tomato and onion approx 10 calories 0% cholesterol 0% fat
Dr Pepper Cherry soda 160 calories 0% cholesterol 0% fat
Sliced 1/3 Avocado 120 calories 0% cholesterol 0% fat
Sour Dough Bread 180 calories 0% cholesterol 1% fat per 2 slices
Salad Dressing 40 calories 1% cholesterol 5% fat
Garlic Shell & Cheese 320 calories 3% cholesterol 17% fat per 4oz
Sliced Fresh Fruit approx 5 calories 0% cholesterol 0% fat

Total 965 calories 4% cholesterol 23% fat

# DINNER

## SPAGHETTI & MEATBALLS

Spaghetti with meatballs and mushrooms, celery, onion mixed up with Garlic and Herb spaghetti sauce. Garlic Bread, small salad and cut fresh fruit for dessert.

Spaghetti 210 calories 0% cholesterol 2% fat per 2oz
Small whole (in a jar) Mushrooms 10 calories 0% cholesterol 0% fat per 6
Garlic Bread 100 calories 0% cholesterol 11% fat per one 2" slice
Garlic and Herb Spaghetti Sauce 80 calories 0% cholesterol 0% fat
Small Salad with Italian Dressing approx 75 calories 0% cholesterol 0% fat
6 pre-made 1 ½" meatballs. 250 calories 14% cholesterol 31% fat
One cup of Sliced Fruit 100 calories 0% cholesterol 0% fat

Total 825 calories 14% cholesterol 44% fat

**TOTAL FOR THE DAY 2190 calories 18% cholesterol 67% fat**

Printed in the United States
By Bookmasters